Artificial Intelligence Applied: The Adoption of AI 2024 & Beyond

Written By: Heath Muchena

Table of Contents

Chapter 1: Introduction - Demystifying Artificial Intelligence

What is AI: Defining the Basics

Artificial Intelligence (AI) is a term that often conjures up images of futuristic robots and intelligent machines in popular culture. However, AI is much more than just a sci-fi concept; it's a field of computer science focused on creating intelligent machines capable of performing tasks that typically require human intelligence. These tasks include learning, problem-solving, perception, and language understanding.

At its core, AI involves the development of algorithms that allow computers to make decisions, often using real-time data. Unlike traditional computers, which follow a predefined set of instructions, AI systems learn from their experiences, adapt to new inputs, and perform human-like tasks.

Evolution of AI: From Past to Present

The journey of AI began in the mid-20th century with the dream of creating machines as intelligent as humans. Early AI research in the 1950s and 1960s focused on symbolic methods and problem-solving. The concept of "machine learning," where computers improve through experience, emerged in the 1980s, leading to significant advancements in the field.

In the 21st century, AI has evolved dramatically, thanks to increased computational power, the availability of large data sets (Big Data), and advancements in algorithms, particularly in areas such as deep learning and neural networks. Today, AI is not a futuristic fantasy but a practical reality, influencing various aspects of our world.

AI in Our Daily Lives: Examples and Impacts

AI's presence in our daily lives is more profound and extensive than many realize. Here are some examples:

- Personal Assistants: AI powers virtual assistants like Siri, Alexa, and Google Assistant, helping us with tasks like setting reminders, playing music, or providing weather updates.
- Online Customer Support: Many online customer support services use AI-powered chatbots to answer queries and provide assistance, offering a more efficient customer service experience.
- Navigation and Travel: AI enhances GPS systems, helping in route planning and traffic management, making our journeys faster and safer.
- Healthcare: AI is used in predictive diagnostics, personalized medicine, and patient care, significantly impacting healthcare outcomes.
- Banking and Finance: AI plays a crucial role in fraud detection, risk management, and personalized banking services.
- Entertainment and Media: From movie recommendations on Netflix to music suggestions on Spotify, AI curates personalized experiences based on our preferences.
- Manufacturing and Production: AI-driven robots and machines are increasingly used in manufacturing for automation, improving efficiency and safety.
- Education: AI is transforming education through personalized learning programs and intelligent tutoring systems.

The impact of AI is multifaceted, offering both opportunities and challenges. While it drives efficiency, personalization, and economic growth, it also presents issues related to privacy, ethics, and job displacement.

As we continue to integrate AI into our lives, understanding its fundamentals, history, and applications becomes essential. This understanding not only demystifies AI but also helps us in making informed decisions about how we interact with this transformative technology.

Chapter 2: Core Concepts of AI - Understanding AI Types

General AI vs. Narrow AI: Definitions and Differences

The realm of Artificial Intelligence (AI) can be broadly divided into two main types: General AI and Narrow AI. Understanding these types is crucial to grasp the scope and potential of AI technologies.

- General AI: Also known as Artificial General Intelligence (AGI), General AI refers to machines that possess the ability to understand, learn, and apply intelligence across a wide range of tasks, comparable to human intelligence. AGI is capable of thinking, understanding, and acting in a way that is indistinguishable from that of a human being. It can transfer knowledge and learning from one domain to another, effectively solving any problem it is presented with. However, as of now, AGI remains a theoretical concept rather than a practical reality.
- Narrow AI: Contrary to AGI, Narrow AI, also known as Weak AI, specializes in one specific area. It is designed to perform a single task or a limited range of tasks with intelligence. Examples of Narrow AI include facial recognition systems, chatbots, and recommendation engines like those used by Netflix or Amazon. Unlike AGI, Narrow AI operates under a constrained set of guidelines and cannot apply its intelligence beyond its specific programming.

The key difference between General AI and Narrow AI lies in their scope and adaptability. General AI mimics the versatile intelligence of humans, capable of applying its cognitive abilities to any problem, while Narrow AI excels in specific, predefined tasks, lacking the broader understanding and adaptability of AGI.

The Role of AI in Problem-Solving and Decision-Making

AI's role in problem-solving and decision-making has grown exponentially, especially in the realm of Narrow AI. Here's how AI is making a difference:

- Data-Driven Decision Making: AI excels in analyzing large volumes of data to identify patterns, trends, and insights that are not easily discernible by humans. This capability is invaluable in fields like business intelligence, where AI-driven analytics can inform strategic decisions.
- Automation of Routine Tasks: AI automates routine and repetitive tasks, freeing up human resources for more complex problem-solving. This is evident in industries like manufacturing and logistics, where AI-driven robots and systems handle tasks like assembly, packaging, and inventory management.
- Enhancing Creativity and Innovation: AI tools also aid in creative processes by providing insights and automating part of the creation process. This is seen in fields like marketing, where AI algorithms can generate content ideas or in design, where AI can suggest design modifications.
- Complex Problem Solving: In areas like healthcare, AI algorithms assist in diagnosing diseases by analyzing medical images or patient data, tackling complex problems that are challenging and time-consuming for human practitioners.
- Predictive Analysis: AI's predictive capabilities are used in various sectors, from forecasting weather to predicting consumer behavior. This foresight aids in making proactive decisions, reducing risks, and capitalizing on future opportunities.

- Ethical and Fair Decision Making: With the rise of AI, there's an increasing focus on developing AI systems that make decisions ethically and without bias. This is crucial in sectors like finance and law enforcement, where biased AI could lead to unfair outcomes.

In summary, AI, particularly Narrow AI, has become an indispensable tool in problem-solving and decision-making across various sectors. Its ability to process and analyze vast amounts of data, automate routine tasks, and provide predictive insights has transformed the way decisions are made and problems are approached. However, the journey towards achieving General AI continues to be a topic of research and speculation, holding the promise of even more profound impacts on problem-solving and decision-making in the future.

Chapter 3: Deep Learning and Machine Learning

Explaining Deep Learning: How It Powers AI

Deep Learning is a subset of Machine Learning, a core technology in AI, that mimics the workings of the human brain in processing data and creating patterns for decision making. It's based on artificial neural networks, which are algorithms modeled after the human brain's structure and function.

- Artificial Neural Networks: These networks are composed of layers of interconnected nodes, resembling the neurons in the brain. Each layer can learn and interpret various aspects of the data, making deep learning exceptionally adept at handling complex, unstructured data like images, sound, and text.
- How Deep Learning Powers AI: Deep Learning allows AI systems to learn and make decisions with minimal human intervention. It's particularly effective in areas like image and speech recognition, where it can identify and classify elements with remarkable accuracy. For example, in facial recognition technology, deep learning algorithms can distinguish individual faces from a vast array of different angles and lighting conditions.

Machine Learning Complexities and Advancements

Machine Learning involves algorithms that allow computers to learn from and make decisions based on data. However, it's not without its complexities:

- Data Dependency: Machine Learning models require large amounts of data to learn effectively. The quality and quantity of this data significantly impact the model's performance.

- Algorithm Complexity: Designing algorithms that can efficiently learn from data is a complex task. It involves selecting the right model, adjusting parameters, and ensuring the model can generalize from the training data to make accurate predictions on new, unseen data.
- Advancements in Machine Learning: Recent advancements include the development of more sophisticated algorithms, such as deep learning, and improvements in computational power. These advancements have enabled the handling of larger datasets and the solving of more complex problems than ever before.

Natural Language Processing (NLP)

Natural Language Processing (NLP) is a field of AI that focuses on the interaction between computers and human (natural) languages. It's at the crossroads of computer science, artificial intelligence, and linguistics.

- Understanding Human Language: NLP involves programming computers to process and analyze large amounts of natural language data. The goal is to enable computers to understand and interpret human language in a way that is valuable.
- Applications of NLP: NLP is used in a variety of applications, including speech recognition systems (like Siri and Alexa), translation services (like Google Translate), and text analysis tools. It's also used in sentiment analysis, which allows businesses to analyze customer feedback and social media comments to gauge public opinion about their products or services.
- Challenges in NLP: Despite advancements, NLP faces challenges such as understanding context, sarcasm,

and idiomatic expressions. The subtleties of human language, including tone and connotation, can be particularly challenging for algorithms to interpret accurately.

In conclusion, deep learning and machine learning are fundamental to the current and future advancements of AI, powering applications from automated customer service to self-driving cars. NLP, as a branch of AI, continues to break barriers in human-computer interaction, making technology more accessible and intuitive. As these fields evolve, they hold the promise of more seamless integration of AI into everyday life, unlocking new potentials and applications.

Chapter 4: Natural Language Processing (NLP)

How AI Understands and Generates Human Language
Natural Language Processing (NLP) stands at the forefront of making human-computer interactions as intuitive as possible. At its core, NLP is about teaching machines to understand, interpret, and generate human language in a meaningful way.

- Understanding Human Language: The process starts with the machine interpreting human language. Techniques such as tokenization (breaking text into words or sentences) and syntactic analysis (understanding sentence structure) are employed. The machine needs to grasp the complexities of human language, including grammar, idioms, and slang.
- Generating Human Language: AI systems, equipped with NLP, can generate human-like text. This is achieved through models like sequence-to-sequence architectures, where the system learns to produce a sequence of words based on the input it receives. This technology powers applications like chatbots and virtual assistants, which can interact with users in a conversational manner.
- Challenges in Understanding and Generation: Despite significant progress, understanding context, tone, and the subtleties of human communication remains a challenge. Similarly, generating language that is coherent, context-appropriate, and engaging is a complex task that continues to evolve.

Applications of NLP

NLP has a wide range of applications that are already impacting various sectors:

- Customer Service: Chatbots and virtual assistants use NLP to understand and respond to customer inquiries, providing quick and efficient customer service.
- Translation Services: Tools like Google Translate employ NLP to provide real-time translation between languages, breaking down language barriers.
- Content Analysis: NLP is used to analyze large volumes of text for sentiment analysis, market research, and social media monitoring.
- Accessibility: NLP technologies enable voice-to-text and text-to-voice conversions, assisting individuals with disabilities.
- Healthcare: In healthcare, NLP is used to interpret clinical notes, helping in patient diagnosis and treatment planning.

Future Potential of NLP

The future of NLP holds immense potential with continued advancements:

- Improved Interaction: Future NLP systems are expected to better understand and replicate human conversation nuances, making interactions with AI more natural and intuitive.
- Cross-Cultural Communication: Advances in NLP will enhance cross-cultural and multilingual communication, making global interactions more seamless.

- Enhanced Personalization: With NLP, AI systems will offer more personalized experiences, understanding individual user preferences and context better.
- Expanding Educational Reach: NLP can democratize education by providing personalized learning experiences and breaking language barriers in educational content.
- Healthcare Advancements: In healthcare, NLP could lead to more accurate patient monitoring and diagnosis by interpreting patient data and medical literature more effectively.

In conclusion, NLP stands as a testament to the incredible progress in the field of AI, bringing us closer to machines that can understand and interact with us in our own languages. As technology continues to evolve, NLP will play a pivotal role in bridging the gap between human communication and machine understanding, opening up new possibilities and enhancing the way we live and work.

Chapter 5: AI and Robotics

Understanding the Integration of AI in Robotics

The integration of Artificial Intelligence (AI) into robotics has marked a significant leap in the capabilities of robots, transforming them from manually programmed machines into intelligent entities capable of learning and adapting. This chapter delves into how AI has become a pivotal component in the field of robotics, and the multifaceted nature of this integration.

- Enhanced Autonomy and Decision-Making: AI equips robots with the ability to make autonomous decisions based on real-time data and sensory inputs. Through machine learning algorithms, robots can analyze their environment, learn from experiences, and perform tasks with a level of independence that was previously unachievable.
- Adaptive Learning: Unlike traditional robots that follow rigid programming, AI-enabled robots can adapt to new situations and tasks. This adaptability is key in dynamic environments where conditions and requirements constantly change.
- Sensor Fusion and Perception: AI empowers robots with advanced perception abilities, combining data from various sensors to create a comprehensive understanding of their surroundings. This feature is crucial in applications such as autonomous vehicles and drones, where accurate environmental perception is necessary for safe operation.

Human-AI Collaboration in Robotics

The synergy between humans and AI-driven robots is creating new paradigms in robotics, known as collaborative or cobots. These robots are designed to work alongside humans, augmenting human capabilities and ensuring greater efficiency and safety.

- Augmentation of Human Skills: Cobots are being used to enhance human skills, taking over repetitive, strenuous, or dangerous tasks, thus allowing humans to focus on more complex and creative aspects of work. This collaboration is evident in industries like manufacturing, where cobots assist in assembly lines without replacing human workers.
- Safe Interaction: Safety is a paramount concern in human-AI robotics collaboration. Advanced AI algorithms enable robots to understand and predict human actions, ensuring safe interactions. This involves real-time adjustments to a robot's movements or actions to prevent accidents.
- Learning from Humans: AI-enabled robots can learn from human behavior and feedback. Through techniques like reinforcement learning, robots can improve their performance based on human input and correction, leading to a more effective human-robot partnership.
- Personalized Assistance: In sectors like healthcare and personal assistance, AI-driven robots are being tailored to provide support that adapts to individual human needs, whether in patient care or aiding individuals with disabilities.

Conclusion

The integration of AI into robotics is a testament to the incredible advancements in technology, opening up new possibilities across various sectors. From increasing productivity in industrial settings to providing personalized care, the collaboration between humans and intelligent robots is shaping a future where the combined capabilities of both are leveraged for greater innovation and efficiency. As this field continues to evolve, the potential for AI in robotics to enhance and transform our lives becomes ever more apparent.

Chapter 6: AI in Healthcare

Revolutionizing Diagnostics and Treatment

The integration of Artificial Intelligence (AI) in healthcare is transforming the landscape of medical diagnostics and treatment. This revolution is characterized by increased accuracy, efficiency, and personalized care.

- Advanced Diagnostics: AI algorithms, especially those based on deep learning, are capable of analyzing complex medical data such as X-rays, MRIs, and pathology slides. They can identify patterns invisible to the human eye, leading to earlier and more accurate diagnoses of diseases like cancer, diabetes, and heart conditions.
- Predictive Analytics: AI systems are used to predict patient risks by analyzing electronic health records (EHRs) and other medical data. This predictive capability is crucial for proactive healthcare management, especially in chronic disease management and preventive care.
- Personalized Treatment Plans: AI is enabling the development of personalized medicine. By analyzing a patient's genetic makeup, medical history, and lifestyle factors, AI can help clinicians devise tailored treatment plans, enhancing the effectiveness of treatments.
- Robot-Assisted Surgery: AI-driven robots are assisting surgeons in performing complex procedures with precision and control beyond human capabilities. These robotic systems can reduce surgery time and improve patient outcomes.

Ethical Considerations

While AI brings numerous benefits to healthcare, it also raises significant ethical considerations:

- Data Privacy and Security: The use of patient data for AI training and analysis must be managed with strict adherence to privacy laws and ethical standards. Ensuring data security and patient confidentiality is paramount.
- Bias and Inequality: There is a risk of AI systems perpetuating biases present in the training data, leading to unequal healthcare outcomes. Efforts must be made to ensure that AI algorithms are fair and unbiased.
- Transparency and Trust: The "black box" nature of some AI systems can be a barrier to trust among healthcare providers and patients. It's crucial to develop explainable AI systems where the decision-making process is transparent and understandable.
- Regulatory and Legal Issues: The integration of AI in healthcare raises questions about regulatory approvals, liability, and compliance with healthcare standards. Navigating these legal landscapes is essential for the safe and effective implementation of AI in healthcare.

Future Possibilities

Looking ahead, the potential of AI in healthcare is immense:

- Expanding Access to Healthcare: AI can help bridge the gap in healthcare access, particularly in underserved and rural areas, by enabling remote diagnostics and telemedicine.
- Advancements in Drug Discovery: AI is accelerating the process of drug discovery and development, potentially reducing the time and cost associated with bringing new drugs to market.
- Integrating Genomics and AI: The combination of genomics and AI holds the promise of breakthroughs in understanding genetic diseases and developing gene-based therapies.

- Continuous Health Monitoring: Wearable AI-powered devices are making it possible to continuously monitor patients' health indicators, leading to more timely interventions and better health management.

In conclusion, AI is reshaping the field of healthcare, offering opportunities for groundbreaking advancements in diagnostics, treatment, and patient care. As the technology continues to evolve, it is imperative to address the ethical, legal, and regulatory challenges to fully realize the benefits of AI in healthcare. The future of AI in this field holds the promise of more accessible, efficient, and personalized healthcare for all.

Chapter 7: AI in Business and Finance

Automating Processes and Decision-Making

In the realms of business and finance, Artificial Intelligence (AI) is a game-changer, significantly enhancing efficiency, accuracy, and profitability.

- Streamlining Operations: AI is instrumental in automating routine and complex processes. In sectors like banking and manufacturing, AI-driven systems handle everything from transaction processing to managing supply chains, freeing up human resources for more strategic tasks.
- Enhanced Decision Making: AI's ability to analyze vast amounts of data quickly and accurately enables businesses to make informed decisions. In the financial sector, AI-driven analytics are used for market analysis, risk assessment, and investment strategy formulation.
- Predictive Analysis: AI's predictive capabilities are a boon for businesses, helping them anticipate market trends, consumer behavior, and potential operational issues. This foresight aids in proactive strategy development and risk management.
- Fraud Detection and Compliance: In finance, AI algorithms are increasingly used for fraud detection, leveraging pattern recognition to identify unusual transactions that may indicate fraudulent activity. Additionally, AI assists in ensuring compliance with complex and evolving financial regulations.

AI in Customer Service and Marketing

AI is transforming the landscape of customer service and marketing, offering personalized experiences and efficient service.

- Personalized Customer Experience: AI-powered recommendation systems in e-commerce platforms analyze user preferences and browsing history to suggest products, enhancing the shopping experience. In finance, personalized investment advice is provided based on individual financial profiles.
- Chatbots and Virtual Assistants: AI-driven chatbots and virtual assistants are revolutionizing customer service, providing instant, 24/7 assistance to customers. They handle queries, resolve issues, and even perform transactions, significantly improving customer satisfaction and operational efficiency.
- Enhanced Marketing Strategies: AI tools analyze consumer data to derive insights about preferences and behavior, enabling businesses to tailor their marketing strategies. This includes targeted advertising, content personalization, and optimizing marketing campaigns for better engagement and ROI.
- Social Media Insights: AI-driven tools mine social media data for sentiment analysis, giving businesses a deeper understanding of public perception about their brand. This insight is vital for reputation management and for shaping marketing strategies.

Conclusion

AI is a powerful tool in the business and finance sectors, offering revolutionary ways to streamline operations, enhance decision-making, and improve customer experiences. As AI technology continues to evolve, its role in these fields is set to become even more integral, promising greater efficiency, accuracy, and growth. Businesses embracing AI are positioning themselves at the forefront of innovation, ready to capitalize on the myriad opportunities this technology presents.

Chapter 8: AI in Daily Life

Smart Homes, AI Assistants, and Consumer Applications

The integration of Artificial Intelligence (AI) into our daily lives is transforming the way we live, work, and interact with our environment. Smart homes, AI assistants, and various consumer applications are at the forefront of this transformation.

- Smart Homes: AI is the driving force behind smart home technology, turning ordinary homes into interconnected, intelligent environments. Smart thermostats learn your preferences and adjust the temperature accordingly, smart lights can be programmed to change intensity based on the time of day, and smart security systems provide enhanced safety by recognizing familiar faces and detecting unusual activities.
- AI Assistants: Virtual AI assistants like Siri, Alexa, and Google Assistant have become household names, helping with a range of tasks from setting reminders to controlling smart home devices. These assistants are continuously evolving, becoming more conversational and personalized, making daily tasks easier and more efficient.
- Consumer Applications: AI is also present in many other consumer applications. Fitness trackers use AI to provide personalized workout and health tips. Navigation apps use AI to suggest the best routes and avoid traffic. Even in entertainment, streaming services use AI to recommend movies and music based on your previous choices.

The Impact of AI on Daily Tasks and Personal Productivity

AI's influence extends beyond convenience, significantly impacting our daily tasks and personal productivity.

- Efficiency in Daily Tasks: AI-powered tools and devices save time and effort. For instance, robotic vacuum cleaners autonomously keep homes clean, and AI-driven kitchen appliances optimize cooking processes, freeing up time for other activities.
- Personal Productivity: AI applications in smartphones and computers help manage emails, schedule appointments, and even track personal goals. These tools help streamline day-to-day tasks, boosting productivity and reducing stress.
- Health and Wellness: AI-driven apps and devices track health metrics like sleep patterns, heart rate, and physical activity, providing insights for a healthier lifestyle. They also offer personalized advice, helping users to stay motivated and achieve their health goals.
- Learning and Development: AI is also making learning more accessible and personalized. From language learning apps to online courses that adapt to your learning style, AI is making education more efficient and effective.
- Social Interaction: AI is enhancing social interaction by making communication tools smarter. Language translation apps break down language barriers, while AI-driven algorithms suggest content that aligns with individual interests, helping to foster communities and connect people.

Conclusion

The impact of AI in our daily lives is profound and far-reaching. It not only enhances convenience and entertainment but also contributes significantly to personal productivity and well-being. As AI technology continues to evolve, it promises to further simplify and enrich various aspects of our daily routines, making life more enjoyable and efficient.

Chapter 9: Explainable AI (XAI) and Ethics

Making AI Decisions Understandable

Explainable AI (XAI) represents a growing area in the field of artificial intelligence, focusing on making AI systems more transparent and their decisions more understandable to humans. This transparency is crucial for trust, accountability, and effective collaboration between humans and AI systems.

- The Need for Explanation: As AI systems increasingly make decisions affecting various aspects of life, the ability to explain these decisions becomes vital. In sectors like healthcare, finance, and law enforcement, understanding the rationale behind an AI's decision can impact public trust and compliance.
- Approaches to XAI: XAI involves developing AI models that include explanatory frameworks. These might be in the form of visualizations of the decision-making process, simplified summaries of the algorithms' functions, or providing 'what-if' analyses to understand how different inputs affect outcomes.
- Challenges in XAI: One of the main challenges is balancing the complexity of AI models, particularly deep learning, with the need for simplicity and comprehensibility in explanations. There's also a challenge in ensuring that explanations are meaningful to different stakeholders, from technical experts to laypersons.

Addressing Ethical Concerns and Biases in AI

As AI becomes more integrated into society, ethical concerns and the potential for biases in AI systems have garnered significant attention.

- Ethical Concerns: Ethical issues in AI encompass a wide range of topics, including privacy, surveillance, fairness, and the impact of AI on employment. Addressing these concerns involves not only technological solutions but also thoughtful consideration of AI's broader societal implications.
- Bias in AI: AI systems are only as good as the data they are trained on, and biased data can lead to biased AI decisions. This is a significant issue in areas like facial recognition, loan approval, and criminal sentencing, where biased AI could reinforce societal inequalities.
- Mitigating Biases: Combating bias in AI involves various strategies, including diversifying training data, employing algorithms that can detect and correct biases, and involving a diverse range of people in AI development and decision-making processes.
- Regulatory Frameworks: Governments and international bodies are increasingly focusing on creating regulatory frameworks to ensure ethical AI development and use. These regulations aim to protect individual rights and promote fairness, transparency, and accountability in AI systems.

Conclusion

Explainable AI and ethical considerations are integral to the responsible development and deployment of AI technologies. As AI continues to evolve and impact more areas of our lives, the importance of understanding, trusting, and ethically managing these systems cannot be overstated. The future of AI, to be beneficial and sustainable, must be guided by principles of transparency, fairness, and inclusivity.

Chapter 10: The Future of AI: Predictions and Trends

What to Expect in the Coming Years

As we look towards the future, the landscape of Artificial Intelligence (AI) is set to evolve dramatically, with emerging trends and innovations shaping its trajectory. Here's what we can expect in the coming years:

- Advancements in AI Capabilities: We'll witness significant improvements in AI algorithms, leading to more sophisticated and efficient AI systems. This includes better natural language processing, more accurate predictive analytics, and advanced robotics.
- Widespread Adoption of AI: AI will become more prevalent across various sectors, including healthcare, education, transportation, and entertainment. This widespread adoption will lead to more efficient processes, personalized services, and innovative solutions to complex problems.
- AI in Personalized Medicine: One of the most exciting developments will be the use of AI in personalized medicine, where treatments will be tailored to individual genetic profiles.
- Autonomous Vehicles and Smart Cities: The coming years will likely see significant progress in autonomous vehicle technology and the development of smart cities, where AI manages everything from traffic to energy use.
- Ethical AI and Regulation: As AI becomes more ingrained in our lives, there will be a greater focus on developing ethical AI systems. This will involve creating frameworks and regulations to manage AI development

and implementation, ensuring it benefits society as a whole.

AI's Role in Shaping Future Societies

AI's influence on future societies will be profound and multifaceted:

- Transforming Workplaces: AI will continue to automate routine tasks, changing the nature of work. While this may lead to job displacement in some sectors, it will also create new job opportunities and demand for new skills.
- Enhancing Quality of Life: From smart homes to AI-driven healthcare, AI has the potential to significantly enhance the quality of life, making everyday tasks easier and healthcare more accessible and personalized.
- Addressing Global Challenges: AI could play a crucial role in tackling global issues like climate change and sustainable development by providing innovative solutions and efficient resource management.
- Education and Learning: AI will transform education systems, providing personalized learning experiences and making education more accessible to diverse populations.
- Ethical and Social Implications: As AI shapes societies, its ethical and social implications will need to be carefully considered. This includes addressing issues of privacy, bias, and ensuring that the benefits of AI are distributed equitably.

Conclusion

The future of AI is not just about technological advancements; it's about how these advancements will integrate into and shape our societies. From revolutionizing industries to enhancing daily life, the potential of AI is enormous. However, it's equally important to navigate this future with a focus on ethics, equity, and the well-being of all members of society. As we step into this AI-driven future, the decisions we make today will set the foundation for how AI shapes our world in the years to come.

Chapter 11: AI and Big Data

Managing and Utilizing Vast Data with AI

In the era of digital transformation, the synergy between Artificial Intelligence (AI) and Big Data is redefining how we manage and utilize vast amounts of information.

- Data Processing and Analysis: One of the most significant roles of AI in the context of Big Data is processing and analyzing large datasets quickly and efficiently. AI algorithms, especially those based on machine learning, can sift through vast amounts of data, identifying patterns, anomalies, and correlations that would be impossible for humans to detect manually.
- Predictive Analytics: AI leverages Big Data for predictive analytics, enabling organizations to make informed decisions based on historical data patterns. This application is particularly prevalent in industries like retail, finance, and healthcare, where predicting future trends can be a game-changer.
- Enhancing Data Accuracy: AI algorithms help in cleaning and validating Big Data, ensuring that the information used for decision-making is accurate and reliable. This process is crucial in minimizing errors and biases in data-driven decisions.
- Real-Time Data Processing: With the advent of AI, real-time data processing and analysis have become a reality. This capability is crucial for applications like fraud detection, online customer support, and monitoring social media activities.

The Significance of Data in AI Advancements

The relationship between AI and Big Data is symbiotic; the advancements in AI are largely driven by the availability of vast datasets.

- Training AI Models: Large and diverse datasets are essential for training robust AI models. The more data an AI system has access to, the better it can learn and the more accurate its predictions and decisions will be.
- Continuous Learning and Improvement: Big Data enables AI systems to continuously learn and improve. As these systems are exposed to more data over time, they become more sophisticated and effective in their functions.
- Diverse Applications: The availability of Big Data has opened up a plethora of applications for AI. From voice recognition in smartphones to advanced diagnostics in medicine, the applications of AI are vast and varied, thanks to the rich data available.
- Challenges and Opportunities: While Big Data offers immense opportunities for AI development, it also presents challenges such as data privacy, security, and ethical use of data. Navigating these challenges is crucial for the responsible advancement of AI technologies.

Conclusion

The combination of AI and Big Data is a powerful force driving innovation and efficiency across various sectors. As we continue to generate and collect more data, the role of AI in managing, analyzing, and deriving insights from this data will become increasingly vital. The future of AI, intertwined with Big Data, holds tremendous potential for further advancements and novel applications, heralding a new era of data-driven decision-making and intelligence.

Chapter 12: AI's Impact on Employment

Will Robots Replace Our Jobs?
The question of whether robots and AI will replace human jobs is complex and multi-faceted. The impact of AI on employment is a subject of extensive debate among economists, technologists, and policymakers.

- Job Displacement: There's no denying that AI and automation have the potential to displace certain types of jobs, particularly those involving routine, repetitive tasks. Industries like manufacturing, transportation, and even aspects of customer service are already seeing this shift.
- Job Transformation: Rather than just job loss, a more common impact of AI is job transformation. Many jobs will evolve as AI takes over certain tasks, freeing human workers to focus on aspects of their roles that require emotional intelligence, creativity, and complex problem-solving.
- New Job Creation: AI also contributes to the creation of new jobs. These include roles in AI development and maintenance, data analysis, and in sectors that are emerging or expanding due to AI advancements, like cybersecurity and AI ethics.

Adapting to the AI-Driven Job Market
The evolving job market demands adaptation from both workers and organizations.

- Skill Development and Reskilling: As certain skills become less in demand due to automation, there's a growing need for workers to reskill and upskill. Learning new skills that are in demand in the AI era, such as digital literacy, AI literacy, data analysis, and soft skills, will be crucial.

- Educational System Transformation: Educational systems need to adapt to prepare future generations for the AI-driven job market. This involves not only teaching technical skills related to AI and data science but also focusing on creative, critical thinking and interpersonal skills.

- Emphasis on Human Skills: Skills that are uniquely human, such as emotional intelligence, creativity, empathy, and complex problem-solving, are likely to become more valuable as they complement AI's capabilities.

- Policy and Organizational Changes: Governments and organizations will need to develop policies and support systems to manage the transition. This includes policies on education, job creation, social safety nets, and ethical considerations around AI and employment.

Conclusion

The impact of AI on employment is not a straightforward narrative of job loss; it's a more nuanced story of job transformation and evolution. While AI does pose challenges to the workforce, it also brings opportunities for growth and innovation. Navigating this landscape requires proactive efforts in education, skill development, and policy-making, ensuring that the workforce is prepared and supported during this transition.

Chapter 13: AI for Social Good

AI's Role in Environmental Conservation and Social Initiatives

Artificial Intelligence (AI) has emerged as a powerful tool not just for commercial and industrial applications but also as a means to address various social and environmental challenges.

- Environmental Conservation: AI is playing a critical role in environmental conservation. For instance, AI-powered systems are being used to monitor wildlife and track endangered species, providing valuable data to conservationists. AI-driven models are also used in climate research, helping scientists predict climate patterns and assess the impact of global warming.
- Social Initiatives: In the realm of social initiatives, AI is being leveraged to tackle issues like poverty, healthcare accessibility, and education. AI-driven platforms can identify regions most in need of aid, optimize resource allocation, and even assist in diagnosing diseases in remote areas where medical resources are scarce.
- Sustainable Urban Planning: AI contributes to the development of smart cities, optimizing traffic flow, reducing energy consumption, and improving waste management, thereby contributing to more sustainable urban environments.

Case Studies of AI Making a Difference

Several case studies highlight the impact of AI in contributing positively to society and the environment:

- Wildlife Protection: AI technologies are used in wildlife reserves to predict poaching activities. By analyzing data from various sources like camera traps and sensors, AI systems can alert rangers to potential poaching threats in real-time.

- Disaster Response and Relief: AI has been instrumental in disaster response. For instance, AI algorithms analyze satellite imagery to assess damage after natural disasters, helping to coordinate relief efforts more effectively and efficiently.
- Agriculture and Food Security: In agriculture, AI-driven technologies are used for precision farming, which involves analyzing soil health, crop health, and weather patterns to improve crop yields and reduce waste. This approach is crucial in addressing global food security challenges.
- Healthcare in Low-Resource Settings: AI is being used to expand healthcare access in underdeveloped regions. Mobile health applications equipped with AI can screen for diseases such as diabetic retinopathy or skin cancer, providing early warnings and guidance in areas where access to medical professionals is limited.
- Educational Tools for the Underprivileged: AI-powered educational tools offer personalized learning experiences to students in underprivileged areas. These tools can adapt to each student's learning pace and style, helping bridge the educational divide.

Conclusion

AI for social good underscores the potential of technology to contribute positively to society and the environment. By harnessing AI for these purposes, we can address some of the most pressing challenges facing our world today. It's a testament to the fact that technological advancements can, and should, be aligned with humanitarian and ecological goals, paving the way for a more sustainable and equitable future.

Chapter 14: Ethical Implications and Privacy in AI

Navigating Privacy Concerns

In an era where data is a crucial component of AI development, privacy concerns have become increasingly significant. The collection, storage, and use of personal data by AI systems raise important questions about individual rights and privacy.

- Data Collection and Consent: The ethical handling of data collection is a primary concern. It's essential that individuals are informed about what data is being collected, how it will be used, and they must consent to this collection and use.
- Data Security and Protection: Ensuring the security of personal data against breaches and unauthorized access is paramount. AI systems must be designed with robust security measures to protect sensitive information.
- Transparency in Data Usage: Users should be informed about how their data is being used by AI systems. Transparency is key to building trust and ensuring that data usage aligns with user expectations and privacy standards.

Building Responsible and Ethical AI Systems

Creating AI systems that are not only effective but also responsible and ethical is crucial for their acceptance and success.

- Incorporating Ethical Principles: The development of AI should be guided by ethical principles, including fairness, accountability, and transparency. This involves careful consideration of the potential impacts of AI on society and individuals.

- Addressing Bias and Fairness: AI systems must be designed to minimize biases, which often stem from biased training data. Regular audits and updates are essential to ensure that AI systems are fair and unbiased in their decisions.
- Regulatory Compliance: Compliance with existing regulations and laws regarding data protection, such as GDPR in Europe, is a necessity. As the field of AI evolves, so too should the legal frameworks governing it.
- Ethical AI Design and Development: Involving ethicists, sociologists, and representatives from diverse groups in the AI design and development process can help in identifying and addressing ethical issues. This approach ensures that AI systems are more aligned with societal values and norms.
- Public Engagement and Education: Educating the public about AI, its capabilities, and its limitations can help in mitigating fears and misunderstandings. Engaging with the public can also provide valuable insights into societal expectations and concerns regarding AI.

Conclusion

The ethical implications and privacy concerns surrounding AI are critical areas that require ongoing attention and action. By prioritizing ethical principles, privacy, and security in AI development, we can harness the benefits of AI while protecting individual rights and fostering a trustful relationship between AI and society. The future of AI should not only be technologically advanced but also ethically sound and socially responsible.

Chapter 15: Comparing the Top AI Applications in the World

Overview of Global AI Trends

The AI landscape in 2023 has been marked by significant trends and developments, with various applications emerging as frontrunners. Some key trends and applications are:

- Retrieval-Augmented Generation (RAG): This approach enhances AI-generated content's accuracy and relevance by blending text generation with information retrieval. It's notably used in enterprise AI for chatbots and virtual assistants, improving their factual knowledge and context awareness.
- Customized Enterprise Generative AI Models: Businesses increasingly favor tailored AI models over general-purpose ones. These customized models cater to specific enterprise needs, from customer support to supply chain management, and offer advantages in privacy and security.
- Need for AI and Machine Learning Talent: The demand for skilled professionals in AI and machine learning continues to grow. This talent is crucial for deploying, monitoring, and maintaining AI systems in real-world settings, a discipline often referred to as MLOps.
- Shadow AI: This refers to the use of AI within organizations without formal IT department approval or oversight, which is rising as AI tools become more accessible. While it demonstrates innovation, it also carries risks related to security, data privacy, and compliance.
- Generative AI Reality Check: As companies move from experimenting with AI to actual adoption, they face practical challenges in implementation. These include

concerns about output quality, security, ethics, and integration with existing systems.

Significance in the AI Ecosystem

These applications and trends signify a rapidly evolving AI ecosystem. They reflect AI's expanding role in enterprise solutions, the importance of customizability, the ongoing demand for specialized AI talent, and the need for governance frameworks to manage AI responsibly. As AI continues to integrate into business operations, these trends will likely shape the future directions and applications of AI globally.

Chapter 16: Artificial Intelligence Applied: The Adoption of AI 2024 & Beyond

The Landscape of AI Adoption in 2024

As we progress into 2024 and beyond, the adoption of Artificial Intelligence (AI) is accelerating across various sectors, reshaping businesses, industries, and everyday life.

- Widespread Business Integration: Businesses across scales and industries are integrating AI to enhance efficiency, decision-making, and customer experiences. From small enterprises to large corporations, AI is becoming an essential component of business strategy.
- Healthcare Transformation: AI is revolutionizing healthcare with advanced diagnostic tools, personalized treatment plans, and efficient patient management systems. The adoption is aimed at improving patient outcomes and streamlining healthcare services.
- Impact on Education: In education, AI is enabling personalized learning experiences, automating administrative tasks, and providing tools for adaptive learning and assessment.
- Advancements in Retail and E-commerce: AI is being adopted in retail for personalized customer experiences, inventory management, and predictive analytics to anticipate market trends and consumer behavior.
- Smart City Initiatives: Urban development is witnessing the adoption of AI in traffic management, public safety, and sustainable resource management, contributing to the evolution of smart cities.

- Challenges and Opportunities: The adoption of AI also brings challenges such as ensuring ethical use, addressing privacy concerns, and managing the impact on employment. However, these challenges are matched with opportunities for innovation, growth, and societal improvement.

AI's Role in Future Society

The future shaped by AI is one of enhanced efficiency, improved quality of life, and new opportunities for growth and innovation. As AI continues to advance, its adoption will play a crucial role in addressing global challenges and opening new frontiers in technology and human capabilities. The journey into 2024 and beyond is not just about technological advancement but also about harnessing AI responsibly for the betterment of society.

Chapter 17: The Convergence of AI with Emerging Technologies

AI and Blockchain

Blockchain technology, known for its security and transparency, intersects with AI to enhance trust and efficiency. AI can analyze blockchain data, improving decision-making in smart contracts, while blockchain offers a secure way to store and manage AI data.

AI in Robotics

Robotics combined with AI leads to more autonomous, intelligent machines capable of learning and adapting. This synergy is revolutionizing industries from manufacturing to healthcare, with robots performing complex tasks more efficiently and safely.

AI and IoT

The Internet of Things (IoT) benefits immensely from AI. AI algorithms process vast amounts of data generated by IoT devices, enabling predictive maintenance, enhancing user experiences, and driving innovation in smart home and city applications.

AI in Virtual Reality (VR) and Augmented Reality (AR)

In VR and AR, AI enhances user experiences by making them more interactive and personalized. AI algorithms can create realistic, responsive environments in VR and enable AR systems to understand and augment the physical world more accurately.

Conclusion

The intersection of AI with these technologies is creating a new realm of possibilities. As these integrations evolve, they promise to transform every aspect of our lives, businesses, and society at large, unlocking unprecedented levels of innovation and efficiency.

Chapter 18: Making Money Online Using AI

Leveraging AI for Online Income Generation

The rise of Artificial Intelligence (AI) has opened up numerous avenues for generating income online. Here are some practical ways to leverage AI for financial gain:

- AI-Driven Content Creation: Use AI tools to create engaging content such as blog posts, articles, and marketing copy. This content can be monetized through platforms like websites, blogs, or social media channels.
- AI in E-commerce and Retail: Implement AI algorithms to optimize e-commerce platforms. Use AI for personalized product recommendations, inventory management, and customer service, enhancing user experience and boosting sales.
- Developing and Selling AI Applications: If you have technical skills, develop AI-based applications or tools and sell them online. This includes apps for image recognition, data analysis, or personal productivity.
- AI-Enabled Market Analysis: Utilize AI for market analysis and trading. AI can help in making informed investment decisions in stock markets or cryptocurrency trading by analyzing trends and patterns.
- Teaching and Consultancy: Offer online courses, tutorials, or consultancy services in AI. As AI is a rapidly growing field, there is a high demand for educational content and expertise.
- Automated Affiliate Marketing: Use AI tools to optimize affiliate marketing strategies. AI can analyze consumer behavior to effectively target products and improve conversion rates.

- Freelancing with AI Skills: Offer your AI expertise as a freelancer on platforms like Upwork or Fiverr. Services can include AI programming, data analysis, or AI system integration for businesses.

Conclusion

AI's versatility makes it a powerful tool for online money-making ventures. Whether through content creation, e-commerce, application development, market analysis, education, or freelancing, AI can significantly enhance online income opportunities. As AI continues to evolve, it's likely to create even more innovative ways to earn money online.

Chapter 19: AI Regulations

Navigating the Complex World of AI Regulations

The regulatory landscape for Artificial Intelligence (AI) is complex and evolving. As AI technologies advance and permeate various sectors, governments and international organizations are working to establish regulations that ensure these technologies are used responsibly and ethically.

- Data Privacy and Security: A primary focus of AI regulation is the protection of data privacy and security. Laws like the GDPR in Europe set strict guidelines for data handling and user consent.
- Ethical Use of AI: Regulations are being developed to address ethical concerns, including biases in AI algorithms, transparency of AI systems, and the impact of AI on employment.
- Sector-Specific Regulations: Certain sectors, like healthcare and finance, have specific regulatory requirements for AI, focusing on accuracy, reliability, and ethical implications.
- Global and Regional Differences: AI regulations vary significantly across different regions, reflecting diverse legal, cultural, and ethical standards. This poses challenges for global AI applications and services.
- Future Regulatory Trends: As AI continues to advance, we can expect more comprehensive and nuanced regulations. This includes potential guidelines on AI in autonomous vehicles, facial recognition technology, and AI in public services.

Conclusion

Understanding and complying with AI regulations is crucial for businesses and developers in the AI space. As these regulations evolve, they will play a significant role in shaping the future development and deployment of AI technologies, aiming to balance innovation with ethical and societal considerations.

Chapter 20: AI Tools and Resources:

Enhancing Your AI Journey

A Guide to AI Tools and Learning Resources

As AI continues to evolve, a plethora of tools and resources have become available to facilitate learning and development in this field.

- Machine Learning Libraries: Libraries such as TensorFlow, PyTorch, and Scikit-learn offer extensive functionalities for building and implementing machine learning models.
- Natural Language Processing: Tools like NLTK and spaCy are essential for developers working on processing and analyzing text data.
- Comprehensive AI Platforms: Platforms provided by tech giants like Google AI, IBM Watson, and Microsoft Azure AI offer a wide range of AI services and tools that cater to various needs and skill levels.
- Data Visualization Tools: For presenting AI data effectively, tools like Tableau and PowerBI are invaluable, offering clarity and insight into complex AI datasets.
- Online Learning: Online platforms such as Coursera, Udemy, and edX provide a plethora of courses covering various aspects of AI and machine learning, catering to learners at all levels.
- Research and Development: For those interested in the latest developments and research in AI, websites like arXiv and Google Scholar are rich resources.
- Community and Collaboration: GitHub hosts a myriad of open-source AI projects, while online forums like Stack Overflow and communities like Reddit's

r/MachineLearning and Kaggle offer spaces for discussion, problem-solving, and networking.

Conclusion

Whether you're a beginner in AI or an experienced practitioner, these tools and resources are invaluable for your journey in AI. They provide the necessary learning materials, development platforms, and community support to enhance your skills and knowledge in this rapidly evolving field.

THE END

www.ingramcontent.com/pod-product-compliance
Lightning Source LLC
LaVergne TN
LVHW051750050326
832903LV00029B/2830